German Bombers of World War I in action

By Peter Cooksley

Color by Don Greer

Illustrated by Ernesto Cumpian

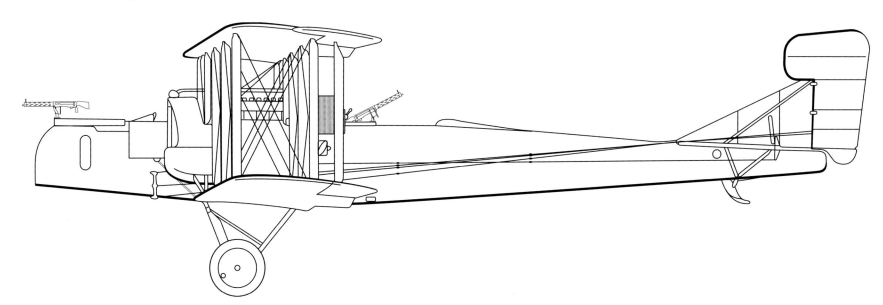

Aircraft Number 173

squadron/signal publications

(Cover) A Gotha G.V (723/17) flies over London on a bombing mission during the spring of 1918. Gothas based in German-occupied Belgium conducted daylight as well as night raids on targets in Britain – including 27 attacks on London – between May of 1917 and May of 1918.

Acknowledgements

In no particular order, the author is most grateful for the loan of photographs to augment his own in this work. The ever-helpful Bruce Robertson; G.S. Leslie, Custodian of the JMB/GSL Collection; and Ray Vann — all members of Cross & Cockade International — and to V.J. Garwood of the Air Historical Society, New Zealand.

Author's Note

The most important of the Kaiser's strategic bombers are dealt with here. Machines which, in most of the warring nations, were ushering in a new use for the aeroplane only thirteen years after the Wright brothers had made it possible for man to fly. From these crude beginnings have evolved the awesome global bombers of today.

ISBN 0-89747-416-3

If you have any photographs of aircraft, armor, soldiers or ships of any nation, particularly wartime snapshots, why not share them with us and help make Squadron/Signal's books all the more interesting and complete in the future. Any photograph sent to us will be copied and the original returned. The donor will be fully credited for any photos used. Please send them to:

Squadron/Signal Publications, Inc.
1115 Crowley Drive
Carrollton, TX 75011-5010

Если у вас есть фотографии самолётов, вооружения, солдат или кораблей любой страны, особенно, снимки времён войны, поделитесь с нами и помогите сделать новые книги издательства Эскадрон/Сигнал ещё интереснее. Мы переснимем ваши фотографии и вернём оригиналы. Имена приславших снимки будут сопровождать все опубликованные фотографии. Пожалуйста, присылайте фотографии по адресу:

Squadron/Signal Publications, Inc.
1115 Crowley Drive
Carrollton, TX 75011-5010

軍用機、装甲車両、兵士、軍艦などの写真を所持しておられる方はいらっしゃいませんか？どの国のものでも結構です。作戦中に撮影されたものが特に良いのです。Squadron/Signal社の出版する刊行物において、このような写真は内容を一層充実し、興味深くすることができます。当方にお送り頂いた写真は、複写の後お返しいたします。出版物中に写真を使用した場合は、必ず提供者のお名前を明記させて頂きます。お写真は下記にご送付ください。

Squadron/Signal Publications, Inc.
1115 Crowley Drive
Carrollton, TX 75011-5010

(Right) Gotha G.III number 398/16 was next-to-the-last G.III built and is covered primarily with unbleached fabric with a gray doped forward fuselage and dark green aft section. The box-like protrusion under the nose is the windshield for the Goerz bombsight.

Go.G.II 388/16

Introduction

Great Britain was separated from the European land mass by the English Channel, a meager strip of water measuring some 22 miles (35.4 KM) wide. That the island nation was a potential target for enemy aircraft was made clear when Louis Bleriot crossed the Channel by air in 1909 — a mere six years after the Wright Brothers made their historic flight in 1903. German awareness of the situation was demonstrated only weeks after the outbreak of war in 1914. Major Wilhelm Siegert submitted to the *Oberste Heeresleitung* (HLL – the German High Command) plans to raid the South-East of England using aircraft flying from Calais. This was a seemingly simple proposition since it appeared likely that the French town of Calais would soon be in the hands of the rapidly-advancing German Army. Progress of the German Army, however, was unexpectedly halted and the intended bombing force was withdrawn to Menz. Despite the disruption of Maj Siegert's plan, Dover was attacked in daylight air raids on 21 and 24 December 1914, and the London docks were bombed on Christmas Day — all by lone, single-engine **Friedrichshafen FF22** floatplanes. These attacks by single-engined aircraft occurred before the introduction of the much-feared bombing attacks by German lighter than air dirigibles, which began on the night of 19/20 January 1915.

There would be nearly two years of German airship raids before a land-based aeroplane raided Britain's capital during the morning of 28 November 1916. Pilot *Deck Offizier* Paul Brandt and *Leutnant* Walther Ilges climbed aboard their single-engine **L.V.G. C IV** (No. 272/16) at Markiakerke near Ostend, Belgium. Their mission was to carry out the most audacious bombing sortie of the war to date. The two men set course for London with the intention of bombing the Admiralty building near Buckingham Palace. For some unexplained reason, the flight of the L.V.G. C IV passed unnoticed by British defenses and arrived over London at 1150 hrs at an altitude of 13,000 feet (3962 M). The two immediately set about dropping the first of their tiny 22 lb (10 KG) high explosive bombs. It is impossible to say whether judgement or luck favored their aim, because the bombs fell between the fashionable shopping area of Brompton Road and Victoria railway station — approximately seven miles (11.3 KM) from the intended target. From that point, the courageous flyers' luck began to run out. Having crossed the town of Hastings on the south coast and headed out over the English Channel without interference, their so-far reliable engine began giving them trouble before finally failing. A forced landing had to be made near Boulogne at 1415 hours. Both Brandt and Ilges were captured.

Coincidentally, during the previous night, a raid on targets in the Midlands by Imperial German Navy Zeppelins (dirigibles) demonstrated the vulnerability of airships as weapons of war. Zeppelin L34, commanded by *Kapitanleutnant* Max Dietrich, was shot down in flames by 2/Lt Ian Pyott flying B.E.2c 2738. A German officer in another Zeppelin recorded: *"The heat of the burning gas made the entire framework red hot.... The fall seemed to last several minutes and we saw her break into two pieces on the sea."*

This was only the latest in a number of lost German airships, the first over British territory was the Schütte-Lanz 11 on 3 September 1916; an action for which the victorious Lt. W.L. Robinson was awarded the Victoria Cross. Despite their great range and load carrying ability, the great airships once feared as the ultimate weapon against which no defense existed was proven to be extremely vulnerable. The hydrogen filled Zeppelin quickly burned when attacked by fighters. During this same period — 1914 through 1916 — aircraft were still unequal to the task of 'long distance' bombing attacks. New methods of carrying out such attacks would have to be found.

Discovering new methods was not difficult; their foundations had already been laid by Igor Sikorsky in Imperial Russia with such giant aircraft as **Le Grand** of 1913 and the **Ilya Muromets** the following year. Nevertheless, the aircraft had to be designed within the limited performance of aircraft engines of the day.

Britain and Italy were not long in following Sikorsky's lead. Britain produced the Handley-Page series of bombers, conceived in December of 1914 with the first prototype flying some twelve months later and becoming operational in March of 1917. In Italy during the same year, the three-engine **Caproni Ca 33** had become standard. The Ca 33's endurance of some three

Gotha G.I 13/15 carried a bomb container under the lower wing center-section. Carbonit high explosive bombs were stored vertically. These early aircraft were regarded as giants due to their wingspan of 66 feet, 7.25 inches (20.3 M). The twin rudders and close set engines helped improve the ungainly looking bomber's single engine performance.

The single A.E.G. G.I — the first of *Allgemeine Elektrizitäts Gesellschaft*'s twin-engine bombers – was built in 1915. It was powered by two uncowled 100 HP Mercedes DI engines. The G.I had a crew of two, consisting of the pilot and the rear gunner.

and a half hours carrying a bomb load of 1000 lbs (454 KG) made possible strategic operations along the Adriatic coast.

Germany too, was alive to the potential of such long-distance weight-carrying multi-engined aircraft with the result that the first Gotha bomber — the **G.II** — appeared, making its first flight in March of 1916. The long dynasty of Gotha bombers began with this design.

The Gotha G.II had evolved from the earlier **G.I**, which had first flown in July of 1915. The G.I, in turn, was an outgrowth of an earlier Fried-Ursinus biplane designed by Hans Burkhard (1889-1977). Burkhard was a prolific Swiss designer who had qualified as a pilot in 1911. He was also to be responsible for the Rumpler monoplane a year later and the Halberstadt-Taube of 1914. Later in life, Burkhard became the technical director of Zurich's Dubendorf airport.

Later versions of the Gotha bomber became so associated with bombing raids in the minds of the British public that the name Gotha became synonymous for any German bomber appearing over London. There were other German bombers deployed during World War One, such as the A.E.G.-built bomber series.

The twin-engined A.E.G. **G.IV** made its first operational appearance toward the end of 1916. The G.IV was the culmination of a whole series of bombers which, due to their lack of load capacity and range, could only be used both as medium-range bombers and as tactical assault aircraft.

Just as the French associated the **Friedrichshafen G.III** with night attacks on Paris, the British associated the Gothas with attacks on London. These Friedrichshafen attacks on Paris began during the opening months of 1917 and continued until the end of the war in November of 1918. The Friedrichshafen G.III could carry a bomb load of 3300 lbs (1500 KG) at a maximum speed of 84 mph (135.2 KMH). The bomb load was triple that of the **Gotha G.V**, which carried up to 1100 lbs (499 KG) at a slightly higher speed of 87 mph (140.1 KMH).

Despite the proliferation of the smaller Gotha, A.E.G., and Friedrichshafen machines, which were revolutionary in their day, two larger German bombers eclipsed these aircraft, the **Zeppelin (Staaken) V.G.O. I**, *(Versuchs Gotha Ost)* and the **V.G.O. II**. The Zeppelin-Staaken V.G.O. I, was a three-engine giant with a wing span of over 138 feet (42 M) and was built for the Kaiser's navy. The V.G.O. I first served on the Eastern Front before being returned to Staaken to have a pair of additional motors fitted. The aircraft later crashed while under test.

The V.G.O I was followed by the V.G.O. II which returned to the three-motor configuration of its predecessor. The V.G.O. II was also used on the Eastern Front before being relegated to training. The V.G.O. II was followed by seven land-plane versions, the most important of which was the Zeppelin (Staaken) **R.VI**.

British arrangements for warning the public of air raids, adequate during attacks by slow-flying Zeppelins, had existed since the earliest days of the war. It was the threat of attacks by faster, fixed winged aircraft which forced the authorities to introduce a new method for warning Londoners beginning in July of 1917. Responsibility for air raid warnings fell largely on the City of London and the Metropolitan Police Forces, the latter caring for an area of 699 square miles (1810.4 KM2) within a fifteen mile (24.2 KM) radius of the Charing Cross section of London.

Audible warning of an impending attack was given by the firing of a pair of maroons (a type of firework used as a warning signal) from 115 selected stations throughout the London area. At first, these were used only up to 2300 hrs; after 14 March 1918, the maroons were used on a 24-hour basis. In daylight the maroons' warnings were augmented by police officers riding bicycles through the streets wearing printed placards bearing the words "POLICE NOTICE. TAKE COVER" and at the same time blowing their whistles to attract attention. A number of automobiles were also used for this purpose.

The all-clear signal, the raiders having passed or been turned back, was given by Boy Scouts who toured the area on bicycles blowing their bugles sounding the Morse Code signal for the letters "CG." The combination had no significance, but gave an easily-identified and simply-given set of musical notes.

The single Friedrichshafen G.I was followed by the smaller G.II. The G.II featured a single fin and rudder versus the more complex biplane tail of its immediate predecessor. Unlike the A.E.G. G.IV, the Friedrichshafen bombers employed a pusher engine configuration.

The Zeppelin (Staaken) V.G.O. (*Versuchs Gotha Ost*) III was the outcome of the earlier V.G.O. I and II machines. The V.G.O. I and II first flew in 1915, but proved to have insufficient power. The appearance of the new machine was deceptive in having *six* engines — two in the nose and two in each nacelle. Each pair of engines turned a single propeller.

Development

A.E.G. G.IV

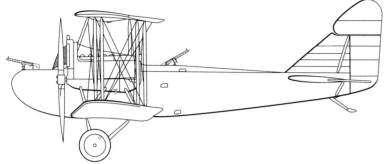

Gotha G.IV

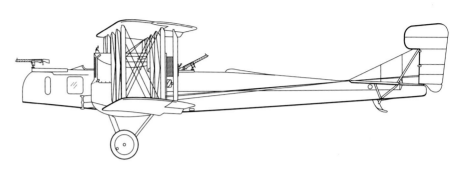

Friedrichshafen G.III

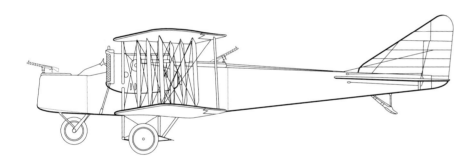

Gotha G.V

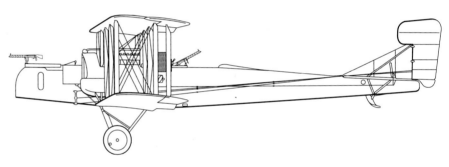

Zeppelin (Staaken) R.VI

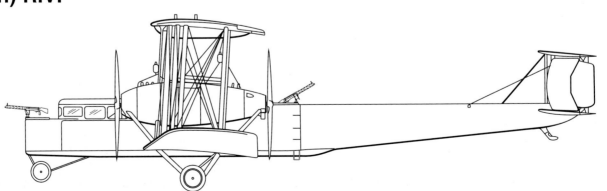

A.E.G. G.IV

The A.E.G. G.IV resulted from the development of A.E.G.'s earlier G-type bombers — the G.I, G.II, and G.III. A.E.G. (*Allgemeine Elektrizitäts Gesellschaft;* General Electric Company of Germany) began to show interest in building twin-engine aircraft in 1914. A single example of the A.E.G. G.1 entered service in early 1915 powered by two 100 HP Mercedes D I engines turning two-bladed wooden propellers. The construction of some 15 to 20 slightly larger G.II twin-engined bombers quickly followed. The G.IIs were powered by two 150 HP liquid-cooled Benz engines, which turned two-bladed propellers. In December of 1915, A.E.G. introduced the G.III, a still larger bomber equipped with two six cylinder, liquid-cooled 220 HP Mercedes D IV engines. The G.III's engines turned four-bladed propellers to take advantage of the increased horsepower. This aircraft was also the first A.E.G. design equipped with balanced control surfaces, a feature which lessened pilot fatigue during long distance flights.

The A.E.G. G.IV had a similar design concept to all three of its immediate ancestors, particularly the G.III. The G.IV had a wingspan of 60 feet, 4.5 inches (18.4 M), a length of 31 feet, 10 inches (9.7 M), and a height of 12 feet, 9.5 inches (3.9 M). Structurally, the G.IV was built of welded steel tubing (unusual by the standards of the time), wood, and fabric. The fuselage was made as a single unit using steel tubing. The nose was covered with plywood, while the remainder of the fuselage was fabric covered. The open crew spaces consisted of a nose compartment, a cockpit, and a rear compartment. The crew had access to all three compartments while in flight. The G.IV could carry up to four crewmembers; however, the normal complement was three. A system for linking the controls provided a second crewmember with a limited ability to fly the G.IV in an emergency. The system only operated the rudder and elevators; it was not connected to the notoriously sensitive ailerons.

The wings employed two steel tube spars with alternating wooden main and false ribs. The leading edges were also made of wood, while the trailing edge was formed using heavy gauge wire — a feature which contributed to the scalloped effect once the wings were covered with shrunken fabric. The tail surfaces were made of welded steel tube and covered with fabric. Although the vertical fin and horizontal stabilizers were given a cambered (curved) surface, the rudder and elevators had a flat surface. Steel tubes braced the vertical fin to the upper fuselage longerons, while a second pair of steel struts connected the horizontal stabilizer to the lower fuselage longerons.

The A.E.G. G.IV was powered by a pair of 260 HP six cylinder, liquid-cooled Mercedes D IVa engines, which were uprated variants of the G.III's 220 HP Mercedes D IV engines. The six-cylinder inline engines were housed in nacelles and joined to the lower wing and fuselage by steel struts. Each engine was equipped with its own radiator mounted at the front of the nacelle. The entire engine nacelle could be completely enclosed; however, the upper panel was usually left off. There were also occasions when the side panels were left off for what is believed to have been a weight saving measure. The missing panels seemed to have little, if any, effect on engine cooling or aircraft streamlining. A unique aspect of the engines was their tractor mounting, with the propellers mounted forward; most German bombers of the era used a pusher configuration with rear-mounted propellers.

The G.IV's main landing gear was comprised of two sets of dual wheels mounted beneath the engine nacelles. The landing gear was fairly standard in its design, apart from using welded steel tube construction and having steel spring shock absorbers. A steel skid served to keep the tail off the ground.

The A.E.G. G.IV's construction employed large amounts of steel, which resulted in an aircraft that was overweight for its size. With a full load of fuel, the G.IV's bomb load of some 880 pounds (400 KG) was meager compared to other German bombers of the era. Light bombs — 25 lbs (11.3 KG) — were carried internally. Two bomb racks were located on the port side

The A.E.G. G.II, which first flew in July of 1915, was slightly larger than the earlier G.I and was built in both twin and triple tail versions. Both G.II versions were powered by 150 HP Benz engines. Some 20 G.IIs were built, with a number serving in operational units. The bombs were carried internally under the cockpit.

of the aft compartment, while a third rack was located beneath the wood flooring between the pilot's cockpit and the aft cockpit. Larger bombs were carried externally. Up to three 100 lb (45.3 KG) bombs were carried under the center fuselage section, while a single 100 lb bomb could be carried under each lower wing, just outboard the wingroot.

The G.IV's defensive armament consisted of two 7.92MM Maxim lMG (*luftgekuhlite Machinen Gewehr* – air-cooled machine gun) Parabellum machine guns. One weapon was mounted on a 360° ring mount in the forward compartment, while the other gun was fitted to a U-shaped mount in the aft compartment. The aft compartment was spacious and allowed the aft gunner to traverse his weapon through a 180° arc around the rear of the aircraft. Each machine gun was fed by drum magazines clipped vertically to the weapon's breech. Additional ammunition drums were stored in the gunners' compartments.

In many respects, the A.E.G. G.IV was not an outstanding design. At 5280 lbs (2395 KG) empty and 7986 lbs (3622.4 KG) fully loaded, the G.IV was overweight for its size. Much of this weight problem can be attributed to the extensive use of welded steel in the bomber's construction. The aircraft was also short-ranged and carried a small bomb load for its size. The bomber was less powerful than the larger 'G' types and was incapable of striking targets in Britain from Belgium. Nevertheless, the G.IV design was said to be capable of absorbing considerable battle damage and the engines, turning airscrews (propellers) without the use of reduction gear, were reliable and sound. German pilots found the G.IV pleasant to fly overall, despite its sensitive ailerons.

The G.IV were mainly used to attack Allied military concentrations behind the front lines. The bombers were assigned to 'Battle Squadrons,' where they provided both offensive and defensive close air support and battlefield interdiction missions. Attacks were made in both day and night, with the day missions usually being accompanied by a fighter escort. Most of these attacks occurred in France, but there were a number of attacks conducted over Macedonia in

the Balkans. The G.IV made a surprise appearance in Macedonia with *Kampfgeschwader* (*KG*; Fighting or Bomber Wing) 1 in February of 1917. KG 1 also flew a single larger and longer ranging Gotha aircraft as well as a number of Friedrichshafen G.IIIs at the time.

The Allies' first real chance to gain technical knowledge of the A.E.G. G.IV came when G.IV G1125/16 was brought down with only minor damage near Achiet-le-Grand, France. Allied pilots reported that the G.IV was largely 'clumsy,' although the lateral stability was praised. Under the numbering system applied by the Allies to all captured enemy aircraft, G1125/16 was allocated the Allied identification code 'G.105.' The designation 'G.105' was mistakenly believed by some to be of German origin. There was no such type as an 'A.E.G. G.105'.

A.E.G. G.IVs are known to have been operated by the following *Kampgeschwaderen* attached to the Armies listed in the given locations: KG 1, Etreux with the 18th Army; KG 3, Ghent with the 4th Army; KG 4, Guise with the 18th Army; KG 5, Mouchin with the 17th Army; and KG 7, la Briquette with the 2nd Army. The following independent *Staffeln* (Squadrons) were attached to the Armies listed: Nos. 1, 2, and 3 (18th Army), Nos. 4, 5, and 6 (17th Army), Nos. 13 to 18 (4th Army), Nos. 19 to 21 (18th Army), and Nos. 22 to 24 (2nd Army).

The A.E.G. G.IV was produced until 1917. Some 542 G-type airframes were produced, with the majority being G.IVs. Siemens-Schuckert also built the bomber under license. Approximately 50 A.E.G. G.IVs were believed to have still been in service by the time of the Armistice on 11 November 1918. Some of these aircraft may have been of the G.IVb, a variant with a wing span increased to 78 feet 9 inches (24 M). The A.E.G. G.IVk was a dedicated ground attack version of the G.IV bomber and was fitted with a .79 inch (2 CM) Becker quick firing cannon in an armored nose. None of the five G.IVks built saw operational service.

Operational A.E.G. G.IIs carried a regular crew of three — a pilot and two gunners. An unusual feature of these designs was the lack of struts linking the engines to the upper wing. The heavily armed G.II was used as a low altitude escort fighter before being relegated to bombing and reconnaissance roles.

The larger and more powerful A.E.G. G.III prototype appeared in December of 1915. It was the first A.E.G. design to have balanced control surfaces. The increased power of the 220 HP Mercedes D IV engines permitted the use of four-bladed propellers. Approximately 45 G.IIIs were built.

Aircrews assigned to *Staffel* 19, *Bogohl* IV display a formidable collection of steel-cased PuW (*Pruefanstalt und Werft* - Test Establishment and Works) bombs. These sophisticated weapons had angled fins to impart a rotation and improve accuracy during their fall. This type of German bombs ranged in size from 27.5 lbs (12.5 KG) to 2200 lbs (1000 KG). An A.E.G. G.IV bomber is parked behind the crews.

Although a rugged aircraft, the earlier G.IV was overweight and carried a small bomb load for its size. The new A.E.G. G.V featured a wing lengthened by some 20 feet (6 M) and a biplane tail to increase the bomb load and improve handling. A trim/servo tab on the ailerons served to reduce aileron loads in flight. A wheeled dolly has been placed under the tailskid to improve ground handling. The bomber is marked G.625 in mid-gray immediately aft of the fuselage cross.

The A.E.G. G.IVb differed little from the G.IV except for a wing span increased by 18 feet, 3 inches (5.5 M) to 78 feet, 9 inches (24 M). The increased span allowed the bomber to carry larger loads. A few G.IVbs also had biplane tails and twin rudders to improve single engine performance. G.168/16 – equipped with a monoplane tail and single rudder – has 'A.E.G.' painted within a rectangular outline under the rudder cross.

The A.E.G. G.IVk was a special ground attack version of the G.IV. The G.IVk featured a biplane tail, twin rudders, and was armed with a .79 inch (2 CM) Becker cannon in an armored nose. Versions of the G.IVk employed both standard G.IV wings and the longer span G.V wings. Five G.IVks were built; however, the aircraft did not see action.

13

Friedrichshafen G.III

Flugzeugbau Friedrichshafen, a branch of the Zeppelin Airship Company, had specialized in a series of single and multi-engine floatplanes of widely varying design and configuration until 1915. That year, Friedrichshafen built the G.I, a three-bay, biplane bomber with two pusher engines. Three-bay biplanes had three sets of wing struts per side (port and starboard). The aircraft was also equipped with a biplane tail and twin rudders. The G.I was followed by the smaller G.II bomber in 1916, which had a conventional tail and two-bay wings. The G.II retained the pusher engine configuration of its predecessor. The aircraft was regarded as moderately successful and was produced in limited numbers. Friedrichshafen G.IIs are known to have replaced the A.E.G. G.IV bombers assigned to *Kampfgeschwader* 1 in 1917. Both the G.I and G.II shared a novel feature in that each of the twin main wheels were equipped with mudguards to prevent stones and debris from being thrown up into the pusher propellers. In some respects, these guards were the forerunners of the FOD (Foreign Object Damage) guards seen on the landing gear of some modern Russian aircraft.

The G.I and G.II were followed by the G.III – the most important of the Friedrichshafen series – in 1917 The new bomber was similar in size and configuration to the G.I; however, the G.III reverted to a conventional tail design with a single vertical fin with rudder and horizontal stabilizers. The G.III had a length of 41.9 feet (12.8 M), a wingspan of 77.7 feet (23.7 M), and a fully loaded weight of 8664 lbs (3930 KG).

The G.III's construction was fairly conventional for the time. The nose and center fuselage sections were built using wood frames with wire bracing, covered with plywood. The aft fuselage section was built using wire braced wood framing covered with fabric. The nose section contained a single compartment mounting a 7.92MM Maxim lMG (Parabellum) machine gun.

The center section formed the heart of the G.III's structure and contained the cockpit, six superimposed cells for internal bomb stowage, fuel tanks, upper and lower wing center sections, and the engines; all forming an interlocking unit. The cockpit employed side-by-side seating for the pilot and *bomben offizier* (Bombing Officer or bombardier), while rudimentary instruments and controls were mounted on the forward bulkhead. Flight control was maintained using a simple yoke and rudder pedals. A fuel tank was also mounted in this section. A small passageway led forward to the front compartment. A second passageway led aft through the center section — containing an additional fuel tank and the internal bomb bay — to the aft gunner's compartment. The gunner's compartment had a trapdoor beneath the floor along with a provision for an extra machine gun. The weapon permitted the gunner to fire at any interceptor attempting to approach under cover of the bomber's 'blind spot' beneath the tail.

The upper and lower center wing sections were built using plywood ribs over two-inch (5.1 CM) steel tube spars. The lower wing's center section upper surface was covered with smooth plywood to improve its load bearing capability, while the remaining upper and lower center sections were covered with fabric. The outer wing panels were built separately using built up wooden spars, plywood main and false ribs, a solid leading edge, and a wire trailing edge. The inboard upper surfaces of the lower wings were plywood covered with the remaining surfaces covered with fabric. The fabric-covered ailerons were made of welded steel tubing.

The interplane struts were built in three pieces. The strut's center, load-bearing section was made of ash, while the strut's leading and trailing edges were formed from softer wood, which was planed and sanded to an airfoil shape.

Both vertical and horizontal tail surfaces were built almost entirely of welded steel tubing and covered with fabric. The horizontal tail surfaces were unusual in having a low aspect ratio; the stabilizer chord (width) was much greater than the span. Additionally, the elevators were

In addition to the new, single tail unit, the G.II introduced two-bay outer wing panels. The oval shapes on the nose were clear panels. Metal guards were mounted behind each **wheel to prevent debris from being thrown up into the propeller arc. Although considered successful, the G.II saw only limited production.**

equipped with a rudimentary device which allowed the pilot to trim the aircraft in accordance with its load.

The landing gear consisted of two pairs of side-by-side main wheels mounted on struts to the wings and fuselage and centered under the engines. Both sets of wheels used steel spring shock absorbers. A fifth wheel was sometimes mounted under the nose to prevent the bomber from nosing over on soft ground. Many bomber missions were flown at night, which always made landing an adventure. An internally sprung wooden tailskid, equipped with a large metal shoe to prevent premature wear, was mounted under the aft fuselage.

The G.III was powered by a pair of 260 HP, six-cylinder, liquid-cooled Mercedes D IVa engines turning two-bladed wooden propellers. The liquid-cooled engines were covered by metal panels and mounted in a pusher configuration. A cutback trailing edge on the center wing section provided clearance for the propellers. A single large radiator was fitted to the front of each nacelle. The engines were nestled between two V-shaped struts. The apex of the 'V' was mounted to the lower wing spars, while the upper ends of the struts were mounted to the top wing spars. Power from the engines provided the G.III with a maximum speed of 83.8 mph (135 KMH).

The Friedrichshafen G.III normally carried two 7.92MM Maxim lMG machine guns. This weapon is more commonly referred to as the Parabellum. One machine gun was mounted in the nose compartment, while the second was carried in the aft compartment. Provision was made for a third weapon, fitted on some G.IIIs, to fire through the trapdoor in the bottom of the bomber's aft compartment. The machine guns were air-cooled and drum-fed; each drum carried 250 rounds of ammunition in non-disintegrating fabric belts.

(Below) The Friedrichshafen G.III reverted to the size of the earlier G.I, but retained the single fin and rudder of the G.II. The three-bay wing form also offered greater range and payload over the smaller G.II. This G.III (628/17) represents the type that formed a significant part of Germany's bomber force between the beginning of 1917 and the end of the war. The printed fabric covering is of the five-color irregular lozenge pattern.

(Above) The Friedrichshafen G.III's Mercedes D IVa engines were mounted on V-shaped struts attached to the two upper and lower wing spars and were braced laterally to the fuselage. G.III 180/17 was given Belgian national markings after being forced down and confiscated from Germany. It was allocated to Belgium's No. 4 Squadron. The lifting marks bear the words 'LEVEZ ICI' (Lift Here). The bomber's fabric covering is similar to that of 628/17.

The G.III's offensive load consisted of up to 3500 lbs (1587.6 KG) of bombs. The largest and heaviest bombs were carried on 12 external racks mounted beneath the fuselage and under the inboard lower wings. Smaller bombs, weighing up to 22 lbs (10 KG) each, could be carried on ten internal racks located within the fuselage center section.

The G.III was soon associated with bombing raids on Paris and the French port city of Dunkirk. The bomber gained rapid popularity among its crews due to its ease of handling, reliability, and general efficiency. The Allies would not be able to examine the G.III in detail until 16 February 1918, when Allied ground fire brought down an example over France. Allied reports on the slightly-damaged G.III dwelt on several interesting features. These features included the mixed construction with plywood covering on the forward fuselage, the four-wheel main landing gear with its coil-spring shock absorbers, and the smaller wheel under the nose to prevent turning over in a rough landing. The reports also noted the unexpected chord to span ratio of the horizontal stabilizer and the internal bomb bay which augmented the 12 external racks.

The G.IIIa was largely identical to its immediate predecessor the G.III; however, the newer aircraft had altered wingtips and reverted to the biplane tail surfaces used on the earlier G.I. The G.IIIa also featured the addition of a 'Gotha Tunnel' in the lower aft fuselage. The tunnel, a Gotha patented design feature built by Friedrichshafen under license, served to improve the

lower gun position's field of fire. G.IIIa bombers were also built by Daimler and Hansa.

The G.IV was introduced in 1918 and resembled the earlier G.IIIa in some areas, particularly the biplane tail. The G.IV's two Mercedes D IVa engines were mounted in a tractor configuration, instead of the pusher layout of previous Friedrichshafen bombers. The nose section was greatly reduced in length from that of the G.IIIa. The shortened nose eliminated the nose gunner's position and machine gun, leaving only the single Parabellum weapon in the rear compartment for defense against enemy fighters. With a wingspan of 74 feet, 2 inches (22.6 M), and a length of 39 feet, 4 inches (12 M), the G.IV was marginally smaller than the G.III and G.IIIa. Both the G.IIIa and G.IV were modified to carry a single large 2204 lb (1000 KG) bomb under the center fuselage section. The increased weight required strengthened landing gear struts and pairing of the main wheels. The pairing doubled the main wheels from four to eight, resulting in an increased ground contact area for the undercarriage. The increased contact area lowered the bomber's ground pressure on soft fields.

G.IIIs were believed to have accompanied the similar-appearing and better-known Gothas on bombing attacks against Britain; however, definite proof of G.III participation in these raids does not exist. Friedrichshafen G.III bombers were active in attacks on Paris and in operations on the Macedonian Front in the Balkans.

Friedrichshafen G.III

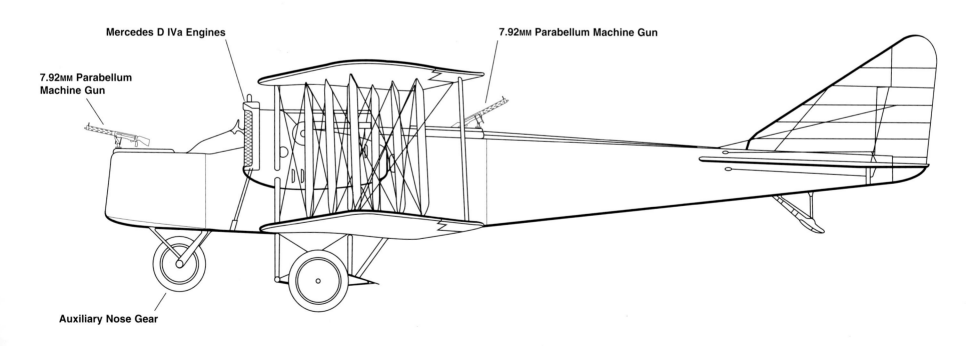

7.92MM Parabellum Machine Gun

Mercedes D IVa Engines

7.92MM Parabellum Machine Gun

Auxiliary Nose Gear

(Below) An unidentified Friedrichshafen G.III coming in to land demonstrates the flat attitude of the G.III in flight. The G.III could carry a maximum bomb load of 3500 lbs (1587.6 KG). Large bombs were carried externally on 12 racks under the fuselage and wing center section, while small bombs were carried internally. The nose wheel, installed to prevent nosing over during night landings, could confuse the identification silhouette.

(Above) The third strut at the end of the wing connected the upper and lower ailerons. The ailerons were made of steel tube covered with fabric. The outer wing panels were largely made of wood with a fabric covering. Wheeled dollys under the tailskid were commonly used by ground crews to maneuver the large aircraft on the ground.

(Below) Some G.IIIs carried a fifth wheel under the nose to improve landing characteristics and prevent standing the aircraft on its nose — particularly at night when the bombers were attempting to land on poorly-lit grass fields. This is an early Friedrichshafen G.III judging from its early style Cross Patee national markings. The number on the fuselage side, difficult to read since it is painted in black on the dark five-color lozenge fabric, is believed to be 118/17.

(Above) In keeping with other German bombers, the Friedrichshafen G.III featured a pair of 7.92MM Parabellum machine guns for defensive purposes. One weapon was mounted in the nose compartment, while a second was placed in the rear compartment. Occasionally, a third machine gun was carried to fire through a trapdoor in the bottom of the fuselage. This G.III is believed to be the same machine shown in Belgian markings on page 15. The prefix Fdh. G.III may be made out just in front of the number 180 on the fuselage. The late German national markings were re-applied on the print — albeit crudely —by an artist.

(Left and Above Left) The captured G.III was well photographed. The front elevation emphasizes the large radiator area provided to cool the two water-cooled, 260 HP Mercedes D IVa engines. Each radiator was equipped with a pair of side shutters to regulate engine cooling. Both the upper and lower wing center sections were cut out to provide clearance for the two-bladed wooden propellers. Again, the national markings, as well as the bracing wires, have been drawn in.

Maxim IMG Parabellum Machine Gun

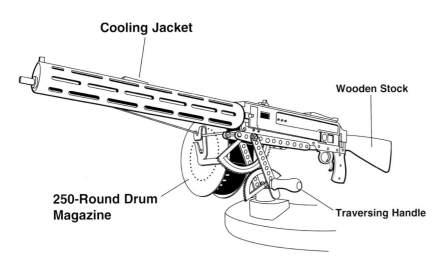

Cooling Jacket

Wooden Stock

250-Round Drum Magazine

Traversing Handle

A Friedrichshafen G.III of KG 5 is inspected by Kaiser Wilhelm II (with walking stick), accompanied by the *Geschwader* commander, *Oberleutnant* Nordmann (pointing). This G.III is fitted with the optional nose wheel. The coil spring suspension is barely visible through the slot in the main strut.

A Friedrichshafen G.III, believed to be 109/15, lies wrecked near Yanesh, Macedonia after being shot down by Lieutenant E. T. Bradley on 8 April 1917. The up-turned ailerons show the light blue dope used on the under surfaces. Nosing over and crushing the nose during night or crash landings was a common occurrence for these bombers.

Seven German officers stand in front of a Friedrichshafen G.III. The shade of the fabric on the fuselage probably indicates an over all dirty white or light blue finish. The fuselage number, painted in black, is Fdh. G.III 1035/16 — Fdh being an abbreviation for Friedrichshafen.

19

(Left) The G.IIIa featured altered wingtips and a biplane tail unit. The tail was first introduced on the G.I, but was deleted on the G.II and G.III. Additionally, the G.IIIa featured a 'Gotha Tunnel,' which allowed an improved field of fire for the lower machine gun. Apart from these changes, the G.III was little different from its immediate predecessor. This G.III was captured by the British and wears red, white, and blue stripes over the rudder. A partial British roundel is painted over the fuselage *Balkenkreuz*.

(Below Left) Another captured G.IIIa, 1429/16 had spurious German crosses added when it was shown in St. James' Park, London some time after the end of World War One. It is known to have been shown in the Imperial War Museum's display of wartime aeronautica during the early 1920s. The vertical tail surfaces are a light color; the surfaces were possibly recovered due to the deterioration of the original fabric.

(Below) The final development of the Friedrichshafen G-series was the G.IV. The G.IV featured tractor mounted Mercedes D IVa engines and a severely shortened nose. The shortened nose deleted the nose gun compartment, leaving the bomber with only a single 7.92ᴍᴍ Parabellum machine gun in the aft compartment. Additionally, the bomber employed a biplane tail unit similar to the one used on the G.IIIa. Due to the bomber's ability to carry a single large bomb — a 2204 lb (1000 ᴋɢ) PuW is visible under the fuselage — the G.IV was equipped with eight wheels. A censor has retouched the area under the tail, obliterating what was perhaps a highly sensitive aircraft ground handling dolly!

Gotha Bombers

Gothaer Waggonfabrik A.G. was the best known German bomber manufacturer; the name Gotha was synonymous with nearly all German multi-engine bombers regardless of their actual manufacturer. Although Gotha built over 20 different single and multi-engine land and seaplane designs over the course of World War One, it is the twin-engined bomber aircraft for which the company was most well known and remembered.

Gotha's first large G-series bomber was the Gotha Ursinus G.U.H. G.1, which appeared in 1915. The G.1 was unique in having the fuselage joined to the upper wing, while the tractor engines and landing gear were placed on the lower wing. The wing and fuselage arrangement allowed the two Benz Bz.III engines to be placed well inboard on the lower wings close to the aircraft centerline. This engine location improved the bomber's single engine performance and handling. Only a few G.1s were built during 1915, followed by a single seaplane variant — the Gotha U.W.D. — in 1916.

The Gotha G.II and G.III bombers made their appearance in 1916. The two bombers were remarkably similar, differing only in their engines and internal details. The G.II entered service in March of 1916 and was powered by a pair of 260 HP, six cylinder, liquid-cooled Mercedes D IV engines mounted in a pusher configuration. Some 15 G.IIs were used in the Balkans until they were withdrawn due to unreliable engines.

The G.III entered service in August of 1916 and was powered by two Mercedes D IVa direct drive engines. Engine power went directly to the propeller shaft without using a reduction gear to reduce revolution speed. Both the G.II and G.III had a wingspan of 77 feet, 9 inches (23.7 M), a length of 38 feet, 8 inches (11.8 M), and weighed approximately 7020 lbs (3184 KG) fully loaded. Both aircraft were armed with two 7.92MM Maxim lMG Parabellum machine guns — one in the nose and another in the aft fuselage — and carried approximately 1200 lbs (544.3 KG) of bombs. A few G.IIs and G.IIIs were equipped with a trapdoor in the undersurface of the rear fuselage, which permitted the rear gunner to take up a prone position and fire aft or downwards from a ventral position to defend the bomber's vulnerable 'blind spot.'

The Gotha G.IV first appeared during the fall of 1916, but does not appear to have conducted regular combat operations until early 1917. The Gotha G.IV and later G.V are the most important of the Gotha series bombers. Both aircraft were similar in layout and design with the G.V being marginally larger, heavier, and faster than the G.IV.

G.IV and G.V fuselages were built as single all wood units with wire bracing and covered entirely with sheet plywood. The G.IV had a fuselage length of 40 feet (12.2 M), while the G.V was slightly longer at 40 feet 7 inches (12.4 M). Both aircraft featured a nose compartment equipped with the bombing controls and a single 7.92MM Parabellum machine gun. The pilot's cockpit was located just beneath the upper wing leading edge. The pilot sat on the left side of the cockpit. A short passageway along the right fuselage side led to the nose compartment. The G.IV's fuel tanks were fitted beneath the wing-mounted engines; those of the G.V were placed immediately aft of cockpit. The tanks completely filled the G.V's fuselage, blocking access to the aft gunner's compartment. The aft gunner's compartment incorporated a unique feature for the time. In addition to the standard Parabellum machine gun mount covering the upper rear and sides of the machine, both the Gotha G.IV and V included a 'gun tunnel.' Gotha had deleted the traditional lower fuselage panel in favor of a triangular section which peaked inside the fuselage. The greatest depth of the tunnel was at the gunner's position. The tunnel's depth was gradually reduced towards the rear of the fuselage until it met the lower fuselage longerons just forward of the tail skid. The gunner aimed his weapon through a slot in the upper fuselage decking and fired through the tunnel. The tunnel permitted coverage of the lower hemisphere in a 25° lateral arc and a 60° vertical arc. On occasion, a third 7.92MM Parabellum machine gun

The prototype of the Gotha Ursinus G.I first flew on 27 July 1915 and was given the serial G.13/15. The aircraft later flew with *Feld Flieger Abteilung* (Field Reconnaissance Flight) 37 late that same year. The G.I carries national markings on both the upper and lower wing upper surfaces.

could be carried in the tunnel position, although this was often at the expense of the bomb load or fuel. The aft gunner's compartment was usually flanked by a pair of formed metal tubes and screens, which formed a protective fence between the gunner and the propellers. The normal crew complement consisted of three men.

Both the upper and lower wings were made using two wooden spars, wooden ribs and leading edges, and wire trailing edges. The wings were made in three sections — two outer panels and a center section. All three sections on the upper wing were fabric covered, while only the lower wing outer panels were covered with fabric. The center section was covered with plywood sheeting on both the upper and lower surfaces. The engine nacelles and bearers were mounted to the lower wing center sections, as was the landing gear. The center section wing chord (width) was reduced on the upper and lower wings to provide clearance for the propellers. Both the G.IV and G.V had a wingspan of 77 feet, 9 inches (23.7 M). The upper and lower wings were swept back at 4° from the leading edge. Ailerons, made of welded steel tube and fabric covered, were mounted on all four wing trailing edges — a feature which contributed to the Gotha's handling and maneuverability. The upper pair of ailerons were balanced to ease control loads. Cabane struts joined the fuselage to the upper wing center section, while additional struts connected the engine nacelles to the outer portion of the upper wing center section. Three pairs of interplane struts joined the upper and lower outer wing sections. All of the struts were made of steel tube with wooden fairings attached fore-and-aft for streamlining. The entire wing structure was wire braced. The tail surfaces consisted entirely of welded steel tubing covered with fabric. The large rudder was equipped with a mass balance at the top to reduce fluttering. The elevators were not balanced.

Both the G.IV and G.V were powered by two six cylinder, 260 HP Mercedes D IVa liquid-cooled engines mounted in a pusher configuration. The Mercedes engines turned two-bladed

wooden propellers that were slightly over 10 feet (3 M) in diameter. The G.IV used large and boxy nacelles, which enclosed both the engine and the fuel tanks. The lower portions of the nacelles were faired into the upper surface of the lower wing. The G.V featured a revised nacelle design. The fuel tanks were moved to the fuselage center section to inhibit fire in the event of a crash, while the engines were housed in new streamlined nacelles mounted between the wings. One or two gravity fuel tanks, primarily used for engine starting, were mounted on top of the upper wing center section. Forty Gotha G.IVs, subcontracted to *Luft Verkehrs G.m.b.H* (LVG), were equipped with 230 HP Hiero engines and supplied to the Austro-Hungarian *Luftfahrtruppe* (LFT – Aviation Troops). All variants employed cooling radiators mounted in the front of the engine nacelles. Additionally, all three variants employed sheet metal cowl panels, although the G.V used fewer panels to expose more engine area to the airstream.

The landing gear was located directly below the engines and consisted of two wheels, spaced approximately six feet (1.8 M) apart. The gear was mounted on V-struts and joined by a transverse axle. Shock absorbing springs were mounted inside the main struts. Wire guards were mounted behind the wheels to prevent debris from being thrown into the propeller arc. A heavy wooden and sprung tail skid, reinforced with steel and equipped with a steel shoe, was mounted below the aft fuselage.

The Gotha G.IV and G.V were each capable of carrying up to 1100 lbs (499 KG) of bombs, although lesser bomb loads were normal. Gothas engaged in missions against England commonly carried a load of six 110 lb (50 KG) bombs for a total weight of 660 lbs (300 KG). The bombs were externally mounted on racks beneath the fuselage and center wing sections inboard of the landing gear.

The G.V was followed by the G.Va, which employed biplane horizontal stabilizers and twin vertical fins and rudders. The effect was to slightly improve single engine performance by placing the rudders in the propeller stream. The later G.Vb retained the G.Va tail configuration and introduced an extra set of twin wheels located in front of the main undercarriage. The Gotha

The high fuselage of the G.I was intended to give a wide field of fire for the defensive gun position. The defensive weapon of choice on German bombers was the 7.92MM drum-fed Maxim IMG (Parabellum) machine gun. The aircraft is coded Go.G.42/15 on the side.

(Above) Four G.Is, believed to be assigned to *Kagohl* (Fighting Wing) 2, *Staffel* (Squadron) 8 on the Western Front during the fall of 1915, wear dark green dope over the fuselages. The G.I on the left still lacks a *Cross Patee* (the curved style cross) on the side, although the white under panel has been added. The national insignia appear under both the upper and lower wings.

(Right) The Gotha G.II was introduced in March of 1916. Approximately 15 G.IIs were used in the Balkans until their withdrawal due to unreliable engines. The bomber (G.II 207/16) has a dark — believed to be black —nose, but is otherwise doped in clear, white, or pale blue. The shadow of the upper wing gives the appearance of a dark color diagonal band across the fuselage.

World War I German Crosses

| 28 September 1914 - 20 March 1918 | 20 March - 11 November 1918 | Alternative 1918 |

(Right) Early Gothas wore the light colored schemes which provided optimal concealment for daylight operations. Later Gothas, new or still serving, began to receive darker camouflage patterns. This captured Gotha G.II wears a five-color irregular polygon disruptive camouflage — the fuselage pattern appears to have been stippled with another color to soften the effect.

23

bombers, like most of the other German twin-engined bombers, spent much of the time operating at night. Night landings proved to cause a large number of accidents; the new wheels were designed to prevent nose-over landings, much like the single nose wheels carried by the Friedrichshafen G.III.

Gotha bomber design and production largely ended with the Gotha G.Vb; however, the company continued to design and produce a small number of large, high speed, twin-engine reconnaissance aircraft: the G.VII, G.VIII, GL.VIII, G.IX, and G.X. All the later aircraft were similarly configured in having short noses — eliminating the nose gun position of earlier Gotha bombers— and having close set engines to improve single engine performance and handling. The G.VII was powered by the stalwart Mercedes D IVa; however, the remainder were powered by 245 HP Maybach Mb IV engines. The G.VII and GL.VIII employed biplane tail assemblies, while the remainder used standard monoplane tails. Defensive armament on all aircraft was limited to a single 7.92MM Parabellum machine gun in the dorsal position. Only a few of each were built and the G.VII, G.VIII, and GL.VIII were the only variants believed to have entered service.

By the autumn of 1916, it became clear to the Germans that the airship attacks on Great Britain were not achieving the expected results. Orders were issued to commence daylight attacks on 1 February 1917; however, sufficient aircraft were not available in time. The first raid on English targets did not take place until 25 May, when 21 Gothas dropped their bomb loads over Dover and Folkestone. Additional German raids followed, the most famous occurring when 17 Gothas dropped nearly 10,000 lbs (4500 KG) of bombs on London on 13 June 1917. The attack killed over 162 Londoners and injured nearly 450 others. The weak British anti-aircraft fire did not hit the bombers, and neither did the sole British aircraft which managed to intercept the German attackers. All of the Gothas returned safely to German-occupied Belgium. The untidy gaggle of 17 Gothas circling over London in broad daylight, and the damage and casualties they caused, aroused the greatest public indignation in Britain.

Daylight Gotha attacks were also conducted against French targets, but over the course of the summer of 1917, Allied ground and air defenses had improved to the point where the Germans began switching to night attacks. *Bombengeschwader* (Bomber Wing) 3, commanded by *Hauptmann* (Captain) Ernst Brandenburg, made 22 night attacks on British towns and cities until May of 1918. The cost to the Germans was high; 24 machines were claimed by British and French air defenses — mainly ground-fire — and 37 more Gothas were written off in accidents. Approximately 30 Gotha G.IVs were supplied to Austria-Hungary during 1917 and were used to attack Italian cities.

(Above) This Gotha G.II, believed to be 204/16, wears the early light colored finish. The national insignia are painted over large white squares on the wings and fuselage. This aircraft has four-bladed propellers and a single wing mounted gravity tank. Barely visible around the rear gunner's position are the wire mesh guards designed to the keep the gunner and gun out of the propeller arc.

(Left) Early Gotha bombers were painted in light colored schemes ranging from clear to white or light blue. Gotha G.II 204/16 is believed to have been doped in the latter scheme, since the original print shows a slight difference in shade between the white background to the fuselage cross and the surrounding fabric. The nose is varnished plywood.

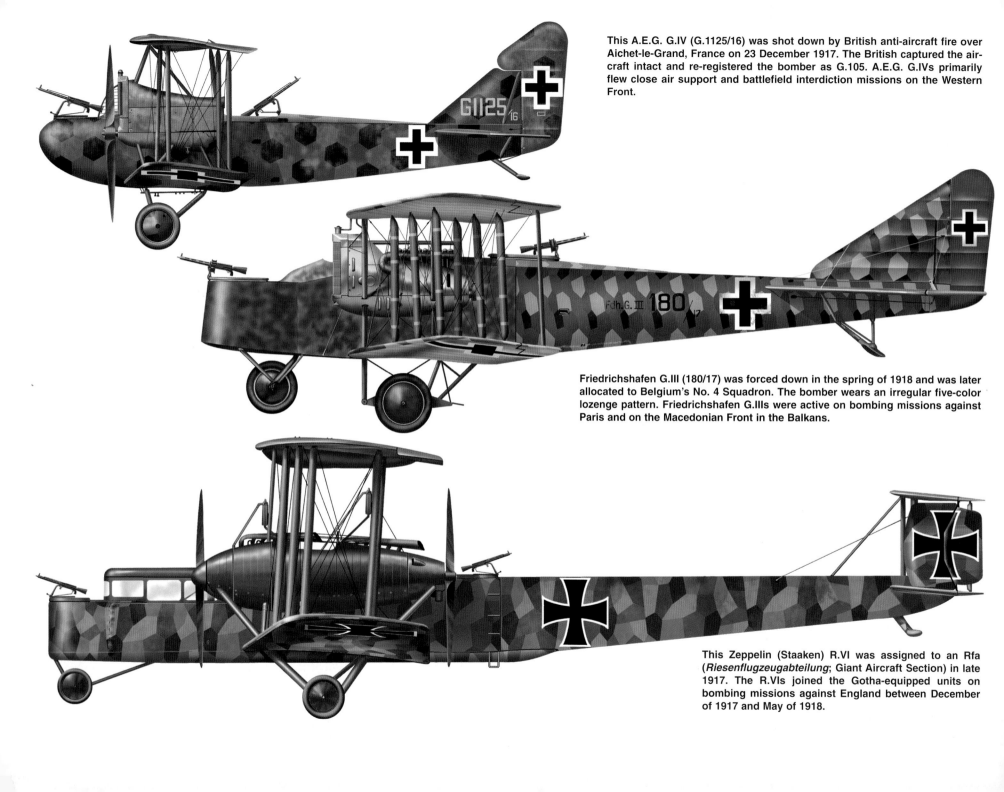

This A.E.G. G.IV (G.1125/16) was shot down by British anti-aircraft fire over Aichet-le-Grand, France on 23 December 1917. The British captured the aircraft intact and re-registered the bomber as G.105. A.E.G. G.IVs primarily flew close air support and battlefield interdiction missions on the Western Front.

Friedrichshafen G.III (180/17) was forced down in the spring of 1918 and was later allocated to Belgium's No. 4 Squadron. The bomber wears an irregular five-color lozenge pattern. Friedrichshafen G.IIIs were active on bombing missions against Paris and on the Macedonian Front in the Balkans.

This Zeppelin (Staaken) R.VI was assigned to an Rfa (*Riesenflugzeugabteilung*; Giant Aircraft Section) in late 1917. The R.VIs joined the Gotha-equipped units on bombing missions against England between December of 1917 and May of 1918.

CIVIL AIR PATROL *Beech T-34 over Long Island; Lt. Col. A. H. Tax, pilot; Dr. B. L. DeClue, co-pilot.*

IGO ETRICH'S *1913 "Taube" (dove) mounted 6-cylinder, 100-hp Mercedes powerplant.*

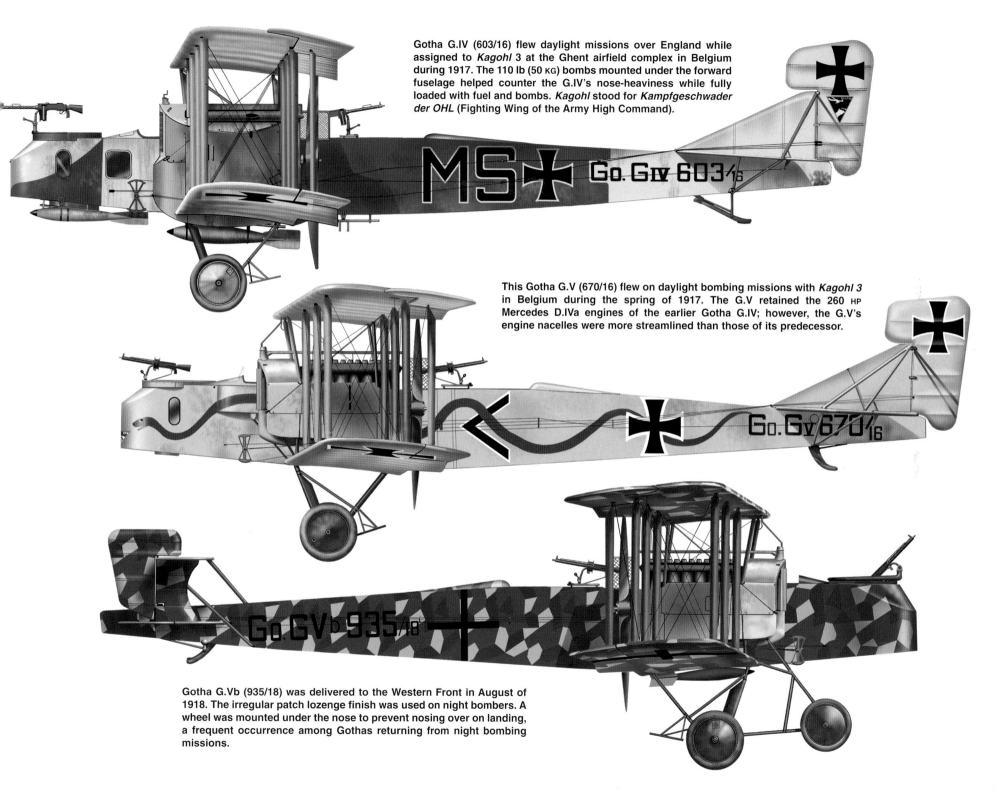

Gotha G.IV (603/16) flew daylight missions over England while assigned to *Kagohl* 3 at the Ghent airfield complex in Belgium during 1917. The 110 lb (50 KG) bombs mounted under the forward fuselage helped counter the G.IV's nose-heaviness while fully loaded with fuel and bombs. *Kagohl* stood for *Kampfgeschwader der OHL* (Fighting Wing of the Army High Command).

This Gotha G.V (670/16) flew on daylight bombing missions with *Kagohl 3* in Belgium during the spring of 1917. The G.V retained the 260 HP Mercedes D.IVa engines of the earlier Gotha G.IV; however, the G.V's engine nacelles were more streamlined than those of its predecessor.

Gotha G.Vb (935/18) was delivered to the Western Front in August of 1918. The irregular patch lozenge finish was used on night bombers. A wheel was mounted under the nose to prevent nosing over on landing, a frequent occurrence among Gothas returning from night bombing missions.

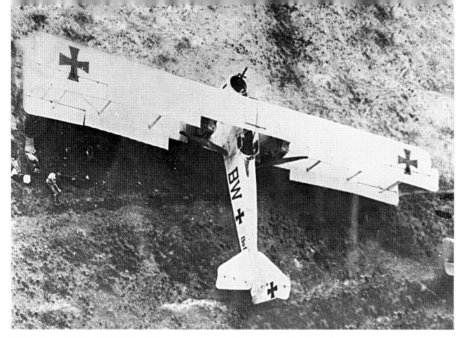

A Gotha G.III of BG (*Bombengeschwader*; Bomber Wing) 3 is parked at its field at Nieuwmunster, Belgium in 1917. The bomber is believed to be in an overall clear-doped finish with black markings. The photograph was allegedly taken through the lower gun tunnel of another low-flying Gotha.

Gotha G.IIIs entered service in 1916, shortly after the G.II became operational. The G.III was similar to the G.II, apart from engines and interior details; however, the G.III remained in service for a longer period of time due to its more reliable Mercedes D IVa engines. This Gotha G.III wears a white/light blue doped fabric. An unusual feature is the lack of canvas covers on the wheels, which provided streamlining over the wheel spokes.

This dark colored Gotha G.III was based on Oesel Island in 1917. A horse-drawn supply wagon is passing in front of the aircraft. Gotha crews operating at high altitude were equipped with Ahrendt & Heylandt liquid oxygen breathing apparatus with individual tubes fed into sound-proof helmets.

Gotha G.III (378/16) was unusual in having the underwing national insignia painted in reverse — a white Cross Patee on a black square. All four wheels are fitted with guards to prevent them from throwing debris up into the propellers.

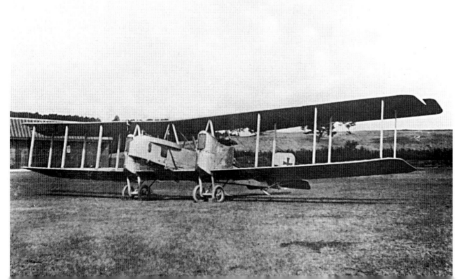

The Gotha G.IV's Mercedes D IVa pusher engines were mounted in large boxy nacelles faired into the upper surface of the lower wing. The nacelles were covered with light alloy panels. A 220 lb (100 KG) PuW bomb is mounted under the nose.

(Below Right) An alternative to firing down the slot in the upper fuselage was to mount a machine gun on the lower position. The ventral position permitted an increase in defensive coverage below and to the rear of the bomber.

(Below) Protective wire guards were mounted around the aft gunner's compartment to keep the gunner and his weapon out of the propeller arc. Both Gotha and Friedrichshafen bombers mounted the guard aft due to the pusher engine arrangement, while A.E.G. G.IVs with their tractor mounted engines carried the guard around the front cockpit. The slot immediately aft of the gun mount allowed the gun to be aimed downward through the gun tunnel. A narrow passageway leads to the pilot's cockpit.

Gotha 'Gun Tunnel'

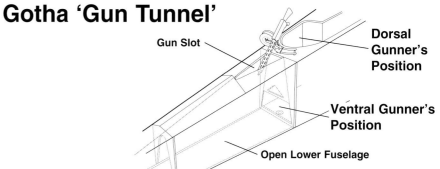

Gun Slot

Dorsal Gunner's Position

Ventral Gunner's Position

Open Lower Fuselage

28

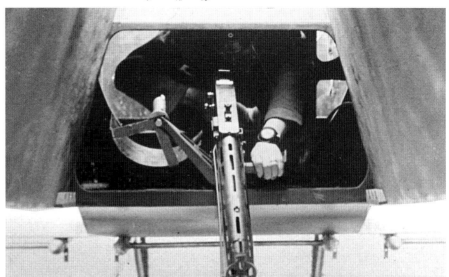

(Above) Gotha G.IV (Go. 408/16) of BG 3 was also photographed from the air at Nieuwmunster, Belgium in 1917. The bomber wears a white/blue finish. The engine nacelles are a dark gray. Two gravity fuel tanks — used primarily for engine starting — are mounted above the upper wing center section.

Maxim IMG Parabellum Specifications

Caliber..7.92ᴍᴍ
Length (incl stock)...............................49.5 inches (125.7 ᴄᴍ)
Diameter of Cooling Jacket (Early).....3 inches (7.62 ᴄᴍ)
Diameter of Cooling Jacket (Late)......1.5 inches (3.8 ᴄᴍ)
Weight...20.9 lbs (9.5 ᴋɢ)
Rate of Fire...700 RPM
Ammunition Capacity...........................250-Round Drum

An artist's impression of the patented Gotha 'gun tunnel' shows the tunnel to be concave. The tunnel was actually more triangular in section, made of plywood, and was some 15 feet (4.6 ᴍ) long. The tunnel ended approximately three feet (.9 ᴍ) short of the fuselage kingpost, the covered vertical strut at the end of the tail.

29

(Below) This Gotha G.IV (believed to have been 660/16) was shot down on 5 June 1917 and crashed in the English Channel on its return home from a bombing raid. The wreck floated long enough for a British ship to haul it aboard for transport to England and a more thorough technical examination. This photo is believed to have been taken two days after the crash while the wreckage was being recovered.

(Above) Souvenir hunters have stripped the wings of this light colored Gotha bomber after it set down at Hartsdown Farm Margate, England at 1800 hrs on 22 December 1917. The bomber suffered engine trouble, forcing the pilot to jettison the bomb load. Incapable of returning to German-controlled territory, the pilot crash landed the Gotha and surrendered. The stripped fabric reveals the wing leading edge, the two wing spars, the built-up ribs, and the internal wire bracing — all common design elements for both Allied and German aircraft during this period.

(Below) A battered Gotha G.IV, claimed to have been shot down by French ace Georges Guynemer, was put on public display in Paris. The parts have been arranged on carts to provide the public with an idea of its size and layout. The clear-doped rudder has a pale ochre shade contrasting with the white background to the Cross Patee and polygon printing on the adjacent fabric. German bombers were regular visitors — during both day and night — to the French capital.

30

The Gotha G.IV's two Mercedes D IVa engines were cowled within large boxy nacelles. A coolant radiator was mounted in the front of the nacelle, while the nacelle bottom housed a fuel tank. The later G.V moved the fuel tanks to the fuselage to reduce the fire hazard and enclosed the engines within smaller nacelles roughly centered between the wings.

Gotha G.IV

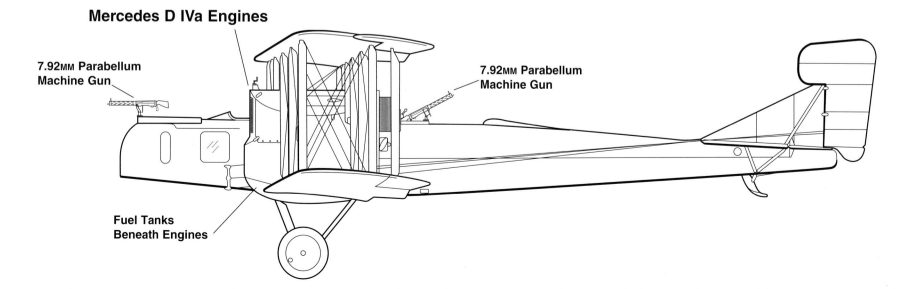

Mercedes D IVa Engines

7.92ᴍᴍ Parabellum Machine Gun

7.92ᴍᴍ Parabellum Machine Gun

Fuel Tanks Beneath Engines

(Above) General Ernst von Hoeppner, Commander of the Imperial German Air Service, reviews the men and machines of *Kagohl* 3 at Gontrode, Belgium. The unit was known as the *England Geschwader* due to its regular 'visits' to England in 1917 and 1918. Additional bomb racks have been mounted beneath the nose of this Gotha. This was a common fitting, which allowed the weight of the bombs to counteract the tail heaviness of the Gotha bombers.

(Below) This early Gotha G.V wears clear dope or light blue finish with natural metal cowlings. The two patches on the side of the nose are windows. Another pair were located on the port side on early Gotha bombers through the G.IV. The G.V featured a bulged cockpit sidewall on the port side, which eliminated the rearmost window.

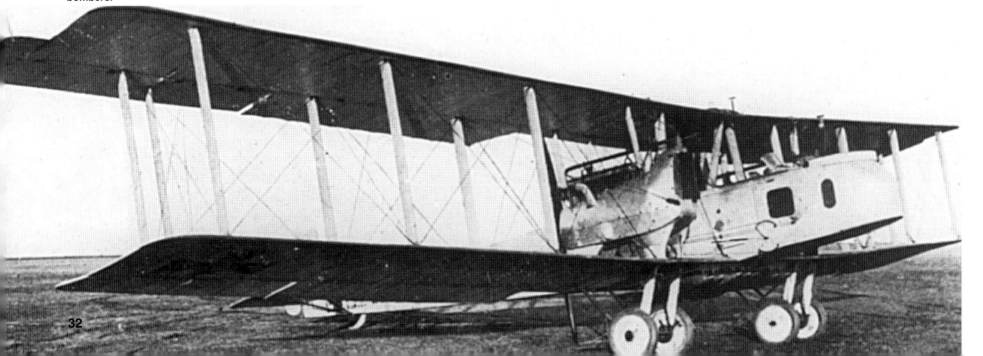

(Above and Below) This early Gotha G.V, believed to be numbered 114/18, has yet to receive its complete national insignia — only the port fuselage and rudder wear the Cross Patee. The bomber appears to be wearing a clear dope finish on the wings and tail surfaces. The translucent dope allowed the internal structure to be visible under certain lighting conditions. The alloy panels on the smaller, more streamlined engine nacelles have been left in a natural metal state. Later Gotha G.Vs were painted a pale blue for daylight operations over the United Kingdom. Gothas began wearing a dark lozenge camouflage pattern when the bombers switched to night attacks over the British Isles. The metal nacelle panels also wore a coat of dark gray paint for night operations.

Gotha G.V

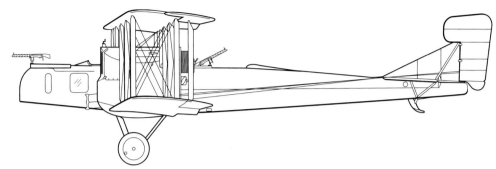

Gotha G.V Right Side

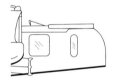

Gotha G.IV

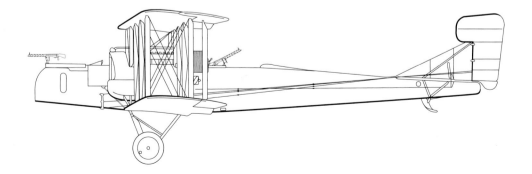

Specifications

Wingspan:.................77 feet, 9 inches (23.7 M)
Length:.....................40 feet, 7 inches (12.4 M)
Height:.....................14 feet, 1.25 inches (4.3 M)
Empty Weight:..........6028 lbs (2734 KG)
Max Weight:..............8745 lbs (3966 KG)
Powerplants:............Two 260 HP Mercedes D IVa in-line
                        engines
Armament:................Two 7.92MM Maxim IMG
                        Parabellum machine guns
Bomb Load:..............660 lbs (300 KG) (varied according to target range)
Speed:......................87.5 MPH (140.8 KPH)
Service Ceiling:.........21,320 feet (6498 M)
Range:......................302 miles (486 KM)
Crew:........................3

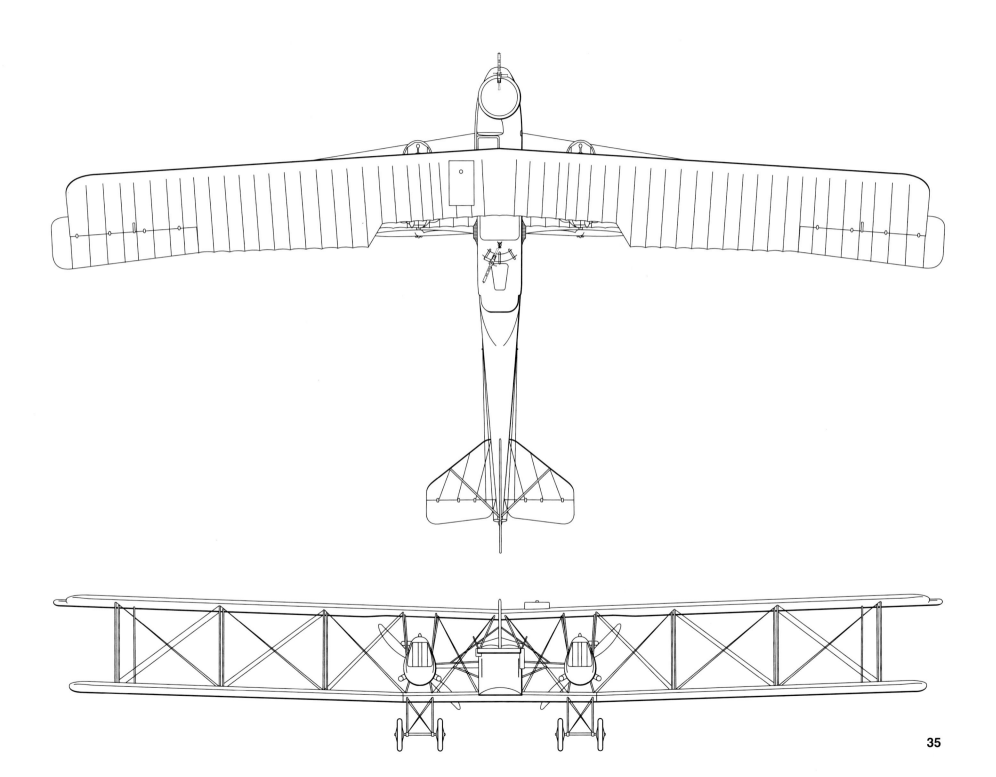

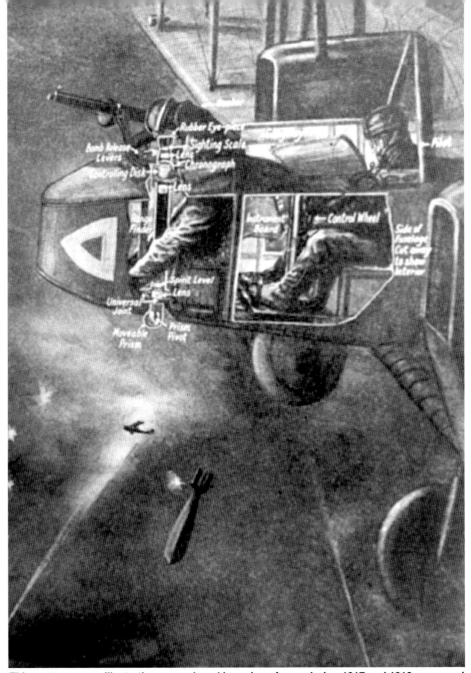

Bomber crews flying at high altitudes were provided breathing oxygen via a simple tube. Early breathing equipment lacked regulators, which resulted in wasted oxygen. Later systems allowed the crewman to adjust the oxygen flow to his needs. The breathing equipment is just visible between the gunner's arm and the breathing tube. 'Pockets' under the rim of the gunring are believed to have held signal flares.

This contemporary illustration, reproduced in various forms during 1917 and 1918, was used to show the cockpit and bomb aimer's position on the Gotha G.II through G.V bombers. The early bombsights were primitive and took into account the bomber's speed and altitude, but not the winds.

Gotha G.V Cockpit

This dark camouflaged Gotha G.V, likely used on night operations, has fallen intact into Allied hands. The rudder has received a set of blue (front), white, and red rudder stripes.

A transparent panel above the Gotha G.V's instrument panel provided light to read the instruments. The airspeed indicator was mounted at left above the naval style compass binnacle. The knobs across the bottom of the panel were fuel valves. The passage at right leads to the bomb aimer/front gunner compartment.

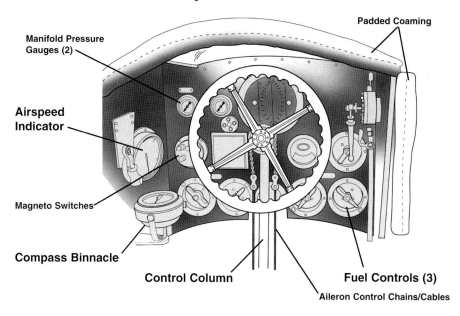

Manifold Pressure Gauges (2)

Padded Coaming

Airspeed Indicator

Magneto Switches

Compass Binnacle

Control Column

Fuel Controls (3)

Aileron Control Chains/Cables

(Below) On 23 April 1917, Lt Breadner of the Royal Naval Air Service (RNAS) brought down a Gotha G.IV (G.610/16). This relatively intact 260 HP Mercedes D IVa engine (No. 29870) was pulled from the Gotha and examined by British technicians.

(Above) The production version of the G.V introduced smaller engine nacelles for the Mercedes D IVa engines. Additionally, G.V nacelles were mounted above the lower wings whereas the G.IV's larger and deeper nacelles had been faired into the lower wing. Brass sheathing protects the leading edges of the wooden propellers. The wings of this G.V appear to be covered with regular hexagon-printed fabric — in contrast to the irregular polygon pattern on the fuselage. The earlier Cross Patee has been altered to the straight-sided *Balkankreuz* form adopted during the spring of 1918.

Mercedes D IVa Specifications:

Length:..................6 ft, 5.5 in (1.97 M)
Height:..................3 ft, 10 in (1.16 M)
Number of Cylinders:...6
Bore:..................6.3 in (160 MM)
Stroke:..................7.09 in (180 MM)
Horsepower:.............260 max, 252 at 14,000 RPM
Cooling:..................Liquid
Propeller..................Wood, Two-Bladed

(Above) A Gotha G.V is loaded with 55 lb (25 KG) PuW bombs. These bombs were usually painted light blue to blend with the under surfaces. Wire cables were used to hold the bombs in place. The double hammerhead device on the fuselage side is the elevator control horn. The aileron control cables lead out of the horn's center. Above and behind the horn are the throttle control rods leading out from under the bulge in the fuselage side.

(Below) PuW bombs were mounted under the wing and fuselage center section. An additional pair of bombs could be mounted under the nose gunner's compartment — a feature which improved the flying characteristics of the tail heavy Gotha G.IV and G.V. The elevator control horn on this G.V is of a slightly different style and is fabric covered. Just in front of the horn is a fairlead for the rudder control cables.

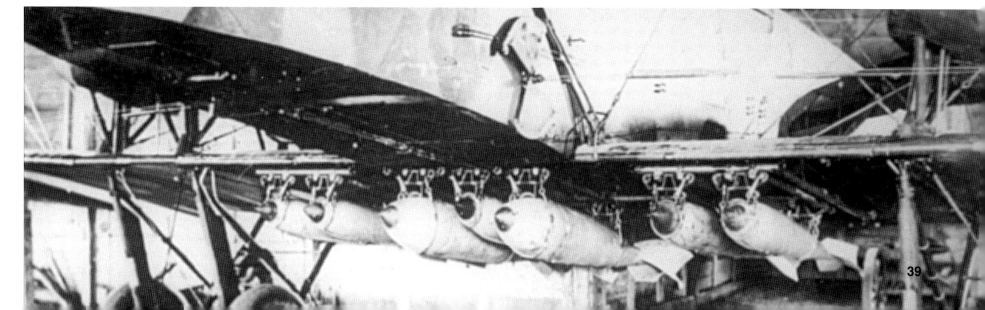

Gothas, wearing a variety of clear and light blue dope schemes, line the field at Nieuwmunster, Belgium. Although its engines have not yet been started, another machine is lined up on the take off area preparing for departure.

The mangled hulk of a Mercedes D IVa engine was pulled from a Gotha G.V which had attempted to land on a golf course after being damaged by ground fire. The Gotha was burnt after the accidental discharge of a flare pistol.

(Above) Gothas taking part in the early daylight attacks on London in 1917 were usually given clear dope or light blue finishes. This is believed to be clear dope with a dark stain over the plywood nose. This G.IV was photographed over Flanders and carries a single gravity tank on the upper wing.

(Below) Gotha bombers were succeeded in production by a number of smaller, lighter, and faster long-range photo-reconnaissance machines, such as this Gotha G.VII (300/18). Defensive armament was limited to a single 7.92MM Parabellum machine gun in the dorsal position.

(Above) Bomb loaders screw the fins onto a 660 lb (300 KG) PuW bomb prior to loading. The bomb's fins were angled to impart a spin, which improved accuracy.

(Above) The Gotha G.VIII resembled the earlier G.VII, but was lighter and had a redesigned single tail unit and longer span wings. The defensive armament remained the same; however, power was provided by a pair of 245 HP, six cylinder, Maybach Mb IV tractor mounted engines. The engines were set near the aircraft centerline to improve aircraft performance in the event one engine had stopped. Only a few Gotha G.VIIIs were built and saw service during the last months of World War One.

(Below) Generally resembling the G.VIII, the further lightened Gotha GL.VIII was equipped with a biplane tail and an additional set of struts to brace the upper wing tips. Defensive armament and engines remained the same. Few GL.VIIIs saw operational service before the Armistice took effect on 11 November 1918. Two additional Gotha designs, the G.IX — built by L.V.G. — and the similar G.X were built; however, neither aircraft was believed to have entered service.

Zeppelin (Staaken) R.VI

The Zeppelin (Staaken) giant bombers were the product of a design team directed by Count Ferdinand von Zeppelin of airship fame. These bombers were the largest aircraft to attack Britain in either of the two World Wars.

The first Zeppelin (Staaken) bomber was the V.G.O. (*Versuchs Gotha Ost*) I, which made its first flight on 11 April 1915. The aircraft was powered by three 240 HP inline, liquid-cooled Maybach Mb IV engines; one was fitted in the nose and the other two were mounted in a standard pusher configuration. The bomber's 138 foot, 5 inch (42.2 M) wing span set the standard for other giant bombers to follow. The next example, the V.G.O. II, was virtually identical to the V.G.O. I and saw action on the Russian Front before being relegated to training.

The V.G.O. I and the V.G.O. II were not regarded as being sufficiently powerful for combat operations. The follow-on V.G.O. III, which saw service with *Riesenflugzeugabteilungen* (Rfa; Giant Aircraft Sections) 500 and 501 on the Eastern Front, was equipped with six 160 HP Mercedes inline engines coupled to drive three two-bladed propellers. The V.G.O. III was succeeded by the R.IV, the first of the series to have the R (*Riesenflugzeug*; giant aircraft) designation. The R.IV retained the six engine configuration of its immediate predecessor, but adopted more powerful 220 HP Benz Bz IV engines in the wing nacelles. These engines turned four-bladed wooden propellers.

The defensive armament for the V.G.O. I through the R.IV ranged from four to six 7.92MM Parabellum machine guns. All four bombers carried gun positions in the nacelle fronts, along with the mid-fuselage station.

The Zeppelin (Staaken) R.V first appeared in 1917; similar to the earlier R.IV, the R.V was powered by five 250 HP Mb IV engines turning four-bladed propellers. The four wing-mounted engines were reversed to a tractor configuration, which relocated the defensive gun positions to the rear of the nacelles. The R.V also introduced the *Schwalbenest* (Swallow's nest) gun position mounted on the top of the upper wing center section, approximately 22 feet (6.7 M) from the main landing gear bottom surface. The R.V was the first of the Zeppelin (Staaken) types to see action on the Western Front, where their size and high ground pressure required operation from specially prepared fields.

The Zeppelin (Staaken) V.G.O.1 through R.V, although impressive aircraft, were little more than single examples of operational prototypes. By 1917, the time seemed right for R types to be put into large-scale production.

The first R.VI (R 25) appeared in June of 1917 and R 26 appeared the following month. Four manufacturers – Zeppelin (Staaken), Schütte-Lanz, Aviatik, and O.A.W. – built a total of 18 R.VIs. All of the R.VIs built were assigned to Rfa 500 and 501, which had been transferred from the Eastern Front to the Western Front during the summer of 1917.

The giant R.VI was uniquely configured among German bombers of World War One. The all-wood, wire braced, and fabric covered fuselage had a cross section resembling that of a bus. In keeping with the established trends, the bomb aimer/front gunner was housed in an open cockpit in the extreme nose; however, the two pilots were fully enclosed within a windowed cabin. Additional space was provided behind the cockpit for a radio operator, navigator, and — it is believed — additional bomb release gear. The center fuselage section held the fuel tanks, while further aft was located a dorsal gun position mounting two 7.92MM machine guns. These weapons were also capable of firing downward through a cutout in the floor. The fuselage was 72 feet, 6 inches (22.1 M) long.

The 138 foot, 5 inch (42.2 M) wing structure was all wood with wire bracing and employed two box-girder main spars and fabric cover-

The V.G.O. III's nacelle mounted engines were mounted pusher fashion, allowing the nacelle fronts to be used as defensive gun positions. The landing gear consisted of six wheels with the tailskid acting as little more than a fender in case of a tail down landing.

(Above) Twin radiators were mounted on the struts above the paired engine installation. Apart from the nacelle gun positions, additional defensive weapons were located in the aft fuselage. The V.G.O. III — sometimes described erroneously as the Zeppelin (Staaken) R.III — saw service with *Riesenflugzeugabteilungen* (Rfa) 500 and 501 on the Eastern Front.

ing. Each wing consisted of a center section and two outer panels. Only the outer panels on the lower wings had a dihedral (upward angle). Unbalanced ailerons, consisting of a steel tube frame covered with fabric, were mounted on the upper wings. All of the struts were made of steel tube covered with plywood fairings for streamlining.

The tail surfaces were built using a combination of aluminum alloy and wood. The biplane horizontal stabilizer span measured approximately 30 feet (9.1 м) — slightly larger than the wingspan of an Albatros D.III or Fokker D.VIII fighter. Both horizontal tailplanes were equipped with unbalanced elevators. The R.VI ini-

(Right) The first of the Staaken giants to be officially described under the 'R' designation was the Zeppelin (Staaken) R.IV. The R.IV was similar to the V.G.O. III, but had more powerful 220 HP Benz Bz IV engines in the nacelles. Two crewmembers were seated in the nose behind the twin engines, while a further pair of crewmen are further aft manning the flight controls. Out on the wing, the gunner conducts his lonely vigil in the port nacelle. The retouched photograph is presumably taken from the starboard gunner's position.

tially employed twin vertical fins and balanced rudders; however, later machines were equipped with three sets of vertical fins and rudders. The outboard rudders were in the propeller stream, which helped their effectiveness, especially if one or both engines on one side were inoperative.

The Zeppelin (Staaken) R.VI was powered by four 245 HP, six cylinder, liquid-cooled Maybach Mb.IVa engines, each turning a two-bladed wooden propeller approximately 13 feet (4 M) in diameter. The 260 HP Mercedes D IVa engine — the engine of choice for the A.E.G., Friedrichshafen, and Gotha bombers — was also used, although the Maybach engines were preferred due to their ability to maintain power at higher altitudes. The engines were tandem mounted within nacelles positioned between the wings. Each nacelle contained a small cockpit between the engines for a mechanic to perform inflight maintenance duties. The metal covered nacelles were mounted to a pair of A-frame support struts anchored to the upper and lower wing spars. Cooling radiators were mounted above each nacelle.

The landing gear consisted of 18 wheels. The main landing gear, mounted beneath the engines, consisted of four pairs of wheels approximately 4 feet (1.2 M) in diameter and mounted on conventional V-shaped struts. Two pairs of wheels were mounted on the port and starboard sides, with a slight gap between the second and third wheel. The complete set of wheels on one side had a wheel track approximately 11 feet (3.35 M) wide. A ninth pair of slightly smaller wheels was mounted under the bomber's nose to improve landing characteristics. The R.VI retained a conventional wooden tail skid with a steel shoe.

The R.VI's defensive armament was comprised of four 7.92MM Parabellum machine guns mounted in the nose and aft fuselage positions. The bomb load varied according to mission requirements and could range up to 4410 lbs (2000 KG). Long range missions – including attacks on the British Isles – had an average bomb load of 2200 lbs (997.9 KG). Bombs up to

220 lbs (99.8 KG) in weight were usually carried internally in the fuselage center section; however, larger bombs — weighing up to 2200 lbs — were carried on external racks beneath the fuselage center section.

The first R.VI attack on the British Isles occurred on 17 September 1917, although the length of the round trip meant that the bomb-load had to be reduced to approximately 2200 lbs in favor of additional fuel. This load consisted of ten internally stowed 220 lb (99.8 KG) bombs; alternately, three 660 lb (300 KG) bombs or one 2200 lb (1000 KG) bomb were externally mounted.

Zeppelin (Staaken) R VI bombers often operated in a mixed force with Gothas on bombing raids against London and other British targets. Eleven attacks were made in this manner by the Rfa between 18 December 1917 and 20 May 1918. R.VI/R39 was claimed to have participated in ten combat missions during this timeframe. The aircraft survived the war, only to be shot down in flames by Polish border troops on 4 August 1919.

The R.VI's value as a bomber – if only by their bomb capacity, which was approximately three times greater than a Gotha's – promoted determined German efforts to further improve the aircraft's capabilities in the final 11 months of the war. These efforts resulted in the appearance of the single R.VII (which closely resembled the R.IV), three R.XIVs (numbered R43 to R45), and three R.XVs (numbered R46 to R48). Both the R.XIV and R.XVs were remarkably similar. Captain A.B. Yaille of No. 151 Squadron, RAF (Royal Air Force), flying a Sopwith F.1 Camel, shot down R.XIV/R43 over Etaples, France on the evening of 23 July 1918. One other Zeppelin (Staaken) machine was believed to have been shot down on 1 August, although

The R.IV and the later R.VII were virtually identical, differing mainly in the arrangement of the struts securing the biplane tail surfaces. Both aircraft, and the R.V, had nearly identical nose sections as well. One possible clue to the identity of this cockpit: the location of the photographer — the photograph appears to have been taken from the _Schwalbenest_ position on the R.V. Both pilots were provided large control wheels and protected from the slipstream by small semi-circular windshields.

The R.V introduced a new engine arrangement for Zeppelin (Staaken) aircraft — a single engine in the nose and two pairs of nacelle-mounted engines now turning four-bladed tractor propellers. The machine gun positions in the nacelles were now at the rear. Defensive coverage for the front of the bomber was provided by the _Schwalbenest_ (Swallow's nest) position above the upper wing center section.

300 KG PuW (*Pruefanstalt und Werft*) Bomb (660 lbs)

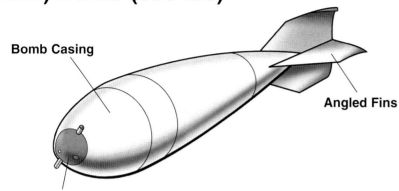

Bomb Casing

Angled Fins

Fuse Assembly

this was described only as 'a five-engine bomber.'

The R.XVs (R46 to R48) were believed to have been produced too late for operational use; however, like the R.XIVs, the R.XVs were of interest in being equipped with five engines. Each engine — three tractor (one in the nose deleting the nose gun position) and two pusher — turned its own propeller. The R.XVs also used the enlarged center vertical fin and rudder introduced on the later R.VIs. A follow-on variant, the R.XIVa, appeared in small numbers and differed chiefly in minor technical details.

The final version of the Zeppelin (Staaken) bombers was the R.XVI (Av), the suffix reflecting Aviatik's earlier experience gained when building six of the earlier R.VIs under license. Power for these aircraft was provided by two of the new 530 HP Benz Bz VI engines and two 220 HP Benz IVa engines. The four engines were paired in tandem (tractor and pusher) in two nacelles and drove individual propellers. These giants were designated R49 to R51. The first R.XVI (Av), R49, was completed in October of 1918, only to demolish its landing gear during a test flight. The aircraft was not believed to have been rebuilt. R50 was completed after the Armistice (11 November 1918) in civilian guise (without armament), although the bomber retained its military lozenge camouflage pattern. The aircraft was eventually broken up after a limited amount of flying. R51 was never completed despite being at an advanced stage of construction.

The Zeppelin (Staaken) R.VI was a remarkable design, powered by four engines paired into two wing-mounted nacelles. Two engines turned tractor propellers, while the remaining pair turned pusher propellers. The R.VI employed up to 16 main gear wheels — mounted in pairs and further clustered into groups of four — to handle the loaded weight of 26,100 lbs (11,836 KG). The R.VI was used in conjunction with the better-known Gothas in attacks on the British Isles in 1917. The irregular polygon pattern of the fuselage camouflage is readily visible and is carried over — in presumably lighter colors — onto the lower surfaces of the wings.

Zeppelin (Staaken) R.VI

The R.VI, with a wingspan of 138 feet, 5 inches (42.2 m), was a massive aircraft for its era. The biplane tail was larger than most single seat fighters of the period. The bus-like fuselage, 16 main wheels, two nose wheels, and the two engine nacelles (themselves longer than most fighters) completed the aircraft. Late production machines had a triangular central fin similar to the later R.XV. This R.VI, believed to be number 28/16, was first used in an attack on England on 17 September 1917.

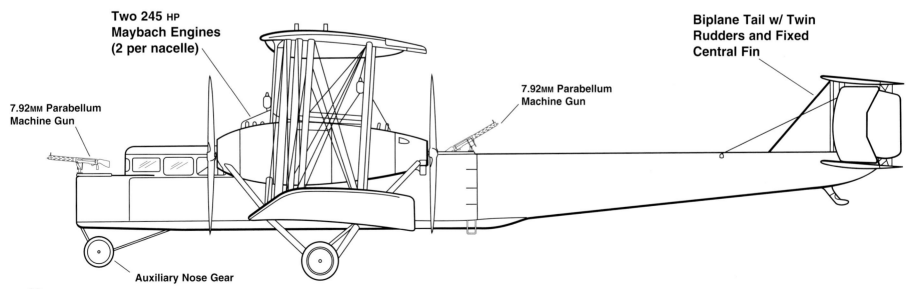

Two 245 HP
Maybach Engines
(2 per nacelle)

Biplane Tail w/ Twin
Rudders and Fixed
Central Fin

7.92MM Parabellum
Machine Gun

7.92MM Parabellum
Machine Gun

Auxiliary Nose Gear

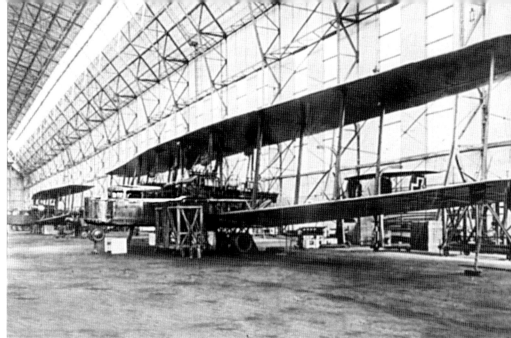

(Above) Most Zeppelin (Staaken) R.VIs were camou-flaged in a dark lozenge pattern for night operations. This R.VI appears to have the fuselage lozenge camou-flage scheme thinly washed over with another shade to produce an undefined hue. The R.VI's size is empha-sized by the men standing around — and in the nose of — the bomber.

(Below) The R.VII was a simple refinement of the earlier R.IV. Apart from some minor modifications to the tail, the two bombers were virtually identical. The R.VII was mar-ginally shorter and lighter in a loaded condition compared to the R.IV. A Zeppelin (Staaken) R.VI is parked in the back-ground.

(Above) Two R.VIs were photographed at the Zeppelin Werke, Staaken bei Berlin during the final phases of their construc-tion. The complete motors have yet to be installed in the machine in the foreground. The two engines in each nacelle were mounted in tandem; the rearmost engine turned the push-er propeller via an extension shaft. The metal tanks flanking the engine bays are believed to have been oil tanks.

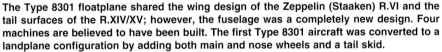

The Type 8301 floatplane shared the wing design of the Zeppelin (Staaken) R.VI and the tail surfaces of the R.XIV/XV; however, the fuselage was a completely new design. Four machines are believed to have been built. The first Type 8301 aircraft was converted to a landplane configuration by adding both main and nose wheels and a tail skid.

The Type 8301's fuselage was suspended between the upper and lower mainplanes, a feature that necessitated the use of a tall nose gear. This aircraft was powered by four 260 HP Mercedes D IVa engines paired in tandem in the wing nacelles and turning both pusher and tractor propellers. The Type 8301 is not known to have proceeded beyond the testing stage.

Zeppelin (Staaken) built three R.XIVs and the identical R.XV in 1918. The bombers were powered by five 245 HP Maybach Mb IV engines and carried up to five defensive machine guns. One R.XIV, R 43/16, was brought down near Etaples, France by Captain Yaille of No.151 Squadron, RAF during the night of 23 July 1918.

On 20 March 1918, the Cross Patee insignia on German aircraft was officially changed to the straight sided Greek or Balkan Cross. R.XIV 45/16 wears her new black crosses, bordered in white, on the rudders and fuselage side. The bomber also appears to have four-bladed propellers mounted on the pusher engines. Both the R.XIV and R.XV were equipped with a large triangular vertical fin joining the fuselage to the upper tail plane — a feature carried over from late production R.VIs.

(Above) The lower wings of the R.XIV/XV series had a slight dihedral. The apparent anhedral on the upper wing is due the angle of the photographer, a mild sweepback on the wing leading edge, and weight on the aircraft. The upper wing was actually flat. All five propellers were given small conical spinners.

(Above) The thin arms on the crosses of R.XV (47/16) are believed to indicate a date after 20 March 1918 — the date the revised crosses were officially introduced. British occupation forces discovered this machine stripped of its fabric on 11 February 1919. Some of R.XV 47/16's parts are believed to have been sent to Britain for detailed study. The bomber was later shipped to Japan; no further information on its fate exists.

(Right) R.XV 48/16 was completed too late for service. Like 47/16, members of the Allied Control Commission discovered it at the Staaken factory in 1919. Despite their nose wheels, the R-series bombers normally sat on their tail skids. Like the G-series, the nose wheels were primarily designed to prevent nosing over during night landings on rough fields.

1069 S.E. 5a

1093 SPAD Fighters

1098 Fokker Dr.1

1123 BE2

More Aircraft of
The Great War
from
squadron/signal publications

1158 Fokker Eindecker

1164 deHavilland DH-9

1166 Fokker D.VII

1171 deHavilland D.H.2